TAEKWONDO

MARTIAL AND FIGHTING ARTS SERIES

Judo

Jujutsu

Karate

Kickboxing

Kung Fu

Martial Arts for Athletic Conditioning

Martial Arts for Children

Martial Arts for the Mind

Martial Arts for People with Disabilities

Martial Arts for Special Forces

Martial Arts for Women

Ninjutsu

Taekwondo

TAEKWONDO

BARNABY CHESTERMAN

Senior Consultant Editor
Aidan Trimble (6th Dan)
Former World, European, and
British Karate Champion
Chairman and Chief Instructor to the
Federation of Shotokan Karate

MASON CREST PUBLISHERS
www.masoncrest.com

Mason Crest Publishers Inc.
370 Reed Road
Broomall, PA, 19008
(866) MCP-BOOK (toll free)
www.masoncrest.com

First printing

1 2 3 4 5 6 7 8 9 10

Library of Congress Cataloging-in-Publication Data on file at the Library of Congress

ISBN 1-59084-391-6

Editorial and design by
Amber Books Ltd.
Bradley's Close
74–77 White Lion Street
London N1 9PF
www.amberbooks.co.uk

Project Editor Chris Stone
Design www.stylus-design.com
Picture Research Lisa Wren

Color reproduction by MRM Graphics, England
Printed and bound in Jordan

IMPORTANT NOTICE
The techniques and information described in this publication are for use in dire circumstances only where the safety of the individual is at risk. Accordingly, the publisher and copyright owner cannot accept any responsibility for any prosecution or proceedings brought or instituted against any person or body as a result of the use or misuse of the techniques and information within.

Picture Credits
Paul Clifton: 11, 30, 37.
Sporting Pictures: 18, 21, 38.
Bob Willingham: 6, 8, 12, 15, 17, 24, 29, 33, 34, 40, 49, 60, 65, 76, 79, 82.

Front cover image: Paul Clifton

Contents

Introduction

When I began studying the martial arts back in 1972, the whole subject was shrouded in mystery; indeed that was part of the attraction. At that time there was only a limited range of books on the subject and therefore very little information was available to the novice.

I am glad to say that this has in recent years changed beyond all recognition. With the explosion of interest in the martial arts and the vast array of quality books that are now on the market, we seem to be increasing our knowledge and understanding of the fighting arts and sports science and this fact is reflected in this new series of books.

Over the past thirty years I have been privileged to compete, train, and teach with practitioners from most of the disciplines covered in this series. I have coached world champions, developed and adapted training methods for people with disabilities, and instructed members of the armed forces in close-quarter techniques. I can warmly recommend this series as a rich source of information for student and instructor alike. Books can never replace a good instructor and club, but the student who does not study when the training is finished will never progress.

Aidan Trimble—Sixth Dan, Former World Karate Champion

Taekwondo is the art of hand and foot. It requires perfect balance and focus to execute techniques effectively. Here, a student of this Korean martial art is performing a jumping attack leading with both his foot and his fist.

The Essence of Taekwondo

For sheer high-kicking, high-flying, gravity-defying action, taekwondo stands out among even the most spectacular martial arts. Fighters leap high into the air, turning, twisting, and spinning to execute exhilarating kicks to an opponent's head. Students learn to condition their hands, feet, and elbows to produce feats of awesome power in breaking wooden boards, tiles, or even bricks. That is taekwondo at its most breathtaking.

As both an Olympic sport and a traditional martial art, taekwondo offers a feast of exciting and impressive moves. Taekwondo students learn to aim high kicks to their opponent's upper torso and head using a variety of different techniques. Whether throwing a front snap kick, a side-piercing kick, a roundhouse kick, or an ax kick, fighters can kick toward any part of the body with equal ease.

There are many different hand techniques to master as well; these techniques are useful when an opponent is too close to kick. Punches, knife-hand strikes, open-handed blows, and elbows can all be used to fend off an attacker or to break boards.

Taekwondo, as with most martial arts, relies on smooth, free-flowing movements to perform its techniques. This picture captures the essence of that freedom of movement as one student attacks another with a jumping front kick that is defended with a high block.

Taekwondo has often been referred to as the Korean karate, but that label does a disservice to this wholly unique and dynamic martial art. Taekwondo differs from karate and other kicking and punching arts, primarily because of its distinctive high kicks and powerful breaking methods. In fact, karate and other arts have, over time, adopted some taekwondo kicks.

Karate is a more commonly known art than taekwondo—particularly among children—thanks largely to the three *Karate Kid* movies. However, those movies actually used a taekwondo expert to choreograph many of the fighting scenes. In the movie world, however, *Taekwondo Teenager* probably would not have had quite the same catchy appeal.

Taekwondo literally means the "art of hand and foot," but it relies heavily on kicking techniques. The legs are three times stronger than the arms and provide a greater reach. It is therefore easier and more penetrative to strike out with your feet rather than your hands. Almost every aspect of taekwondo, from stances to patterns to **sparring**, is designed to increase power in the legs so that students are ready to perform its difficult high kicks.

A BIT OF HISTORY

Taekwondo is a Korean martial art. Although it was officially declared a martial art in 1955, its origins can be traced back almost 2,000 years, to the Koguryo Dynasty, to drawings on the ceiling of a royal tomb that appear to depict fighters in a taekwondo contest. In another tomb, a drawing of two wrestlers, presumably competing in a **cireum** (the traditional Korean form of wrestling) match was found. These early fighting methods are said to have originated from five principles laid out by a Buddhist monk named Wong Kwang: be loyal to your king; be obedient

Grand Master General Choi Hong Hi—the father of modern taekwondo—devoted his life to studying ancient Korean and Japanese martial arts before creating the official martial art of Korea in 1955.

Taekwondo differs from other Korean martial arts, such as hapkido (shown here), which is similar to the Japanese art of aikido and uses techniques such as wrist locks, which are not permitted in taekwondo.

to your parents; be honorable to your friends; never retreat in battle; and kill with justice.

Ancient Korea at this time was divided up into three kingdoms: Koguryo in the north, Baekchae in the west, and Silla in the southeast. Silla was the smallest of the three kingdoms and lived in constant fear of being overrun by its larger neighbors. In the sixth century, the King of Silla, Ching-Hung, organized an army of young warriors called the **hwarang** (translated as "the flowering manhood") to protect his kingdom. These warriors were trained in the ancient open-handed martial arts of **taekyon** (foot fighting) and **subak**. They formed a formidable fighting force, and their style became known as hwarangdo, or "way of the flowering manhood."

Martial arts remained popular in Korea for hundreds of years until the country went through a period of antimilitary rule. Even then, however, they were still practiced daily by the masses. Then, in 1909, Japan **annexed** Korea, banned all traditional martial arts, and forced students to take up Japanese martial arts, such as karate, judo, and jujutsu. Korean arts survived, however; some people practiced them in secret, while other martial artists fled to China.

After Korea was liberated from Japan in 1945, the government made a special effort to rekindle interest in the traditional arts. It sought to unify them under a single Korean art form in an effort to revitalize the traditional art of subak. In the meantime, an army general, Grand Master Choi Hong Hi, had begun a quest to research martial arts in 1938, when he had gone to Japan to learn karate. General Choi had been a student of taekyon in Korea before going to Japan. After attaining a 2nd **dan** black belt in karate, he returned to Korea to complete his taekyon studies. General Choi drew on influences from taekyon, subak, and karate to create taekwondo. Seventeen years later, his diligent research eventually culminated in the formal recognition of taekwondo as the official martial art of Korea at a special conference on April 11, 1955.

A UNIFIED KOREAN ART

Not all of the Korean martial arts merged into the Korean Taekwondo Association (KTA) to form the new style called taekwondo. Those that chose to stay out of the unified arts still exist today, although with a much smaller number of practitioners than taekwondo. Tang soo do, which means "way of the Chinese fist," remained separate, even though it is similar to taekwondo. Tang soo do differs slightly from taekwondo in that it uses big, circular kicks and long hand strikes, like the Chinese arts. It is based on the principle that greater power can be achieved at the point of maximum extension of either the arm or the leg.

As the name "way of the Chinese fist" suggests, tang soo do was influenced by the Chinese arts. This is because its founder, Hwang Kee, escaped to China during the Japanese occupation and picked up ideas from his adopted country. In fact, all Korean martial arts are influenced by Chinese, Japanese, or Mongolian martial arts in some way.

Hapkido, which means "way of harmony," is another art that chose to remain separate from the unified association. Hapkido is similar to both **aikido** and jujutsu, but it also includes breaking techniques similar to those used in taekwondo and tang soo do (these techniques are common only in indigenous Korean martial arts). The hapkido headquarters was set up in the U.S. In fact, hapkido was one of the first martial arts to be

Tang soo do, another Korean martial art, is similar to taekwondo, but it derives more influences from the long, straight, circular techniques of Chinese martial arts rather than the shorter, sharper blows common in Japanese arts.

introduced to the Western world. It was introduced through the 1972 movie called *Billy Jack*, which featured scenes depicting actors fighting using hapkido techniques.

Both tang soo do and hapkido remain popular in Korea, although taekwondo is the official national martial art. Cireum, which derives influences from Mongolian wrestling, is also quite popular. Freestyle wrestling and judo are popular as well, and the Koreans have produced several Olympic champions in both.

THE SPREAD OF TAEKWONDO AROUND THE WORLD

As soon as it became the national martial art, taekwondo was quickly introduced into military training, and then into universities and high schools. General Choi also dispatched demonstration teams all over the world to introduce the new Korean fighting art. Master Jhoon Rhee introduced taekwondo to the U.S. in 1956 when he attended Southwest Texas State University in San Marcos. He set up the first public taekwondo club in San Marcos in 1958. Taekwondo was also introduced to Vietnamese soldiers in 1962, as it quickly began to spread across the world. Master Rhee and Grand Master Rhee Ki Ha, who introduced taekwondo to Great Britain, are credited with the spread of taekwondo's popularity in the West. Along with General Choi, both still travel today, promoting taekwondo around the world.

Although General Choi was the founder of taekwondo and president of the KTA, he fell out with the Korean government over the direction the KTA was taking and resigned from his presidency. His emphasis was on taekwondo as self-defense rather than a sport. In 1966, he founded the International Taekwondo Federation (ITF), which he eventually moved to Montreal, Canada. The new KTA president felt that the world-governing body of taekwondo should be located in its mother country, so he responded by dissolving connections between the KTA and the ITF and set up a rival body, the World Taekwondo Federation (WTF), which was headquartered in Korea, where it remains to this day. Since then, two rival styles have existed in taekwondo, and each has adopted different competition rules. It is the WTF style, however, that the International Olympic Committee (IOC) recognizes.

Taekwondo became an official Olympic sport for the first time at the Games in Sydney in 2000. The International Olympic Committee recognizes the full-contact rules laid down by the World Taekwondo Federation, which uses full body protectors in competition.

AN OLYMPIC SPORT

Despite this split within taekwondo, it is still a less fragmented martial art than karate. This is exactly the reason why taekwondo became an Olympic sport rather than karate.

Taekwondo was first introduced as a demonstration event at the 1988 Olympics in Seoul, but it did not make it on the official Olympic calendar until the 2000 Olympics in Sydney. Despite being the newest Olympic sport, taekwondo burst onto the scene on the first day of competition, when

As taekwondo is the official martial art of Korea, it is included in the national curriculum at schools. Practice sessions at some schools can cater to hundreds of students at the same time.

Cynthia Cameron of Australia won an unexpected gold medal in front of her home crowd. The sport made further news the next day when Tran Hieu Ngan became Vietnam's first ever Olympic medalist.

As an Olympic sport, taekwondo is explosive and electrifying. However, the principles set out by General Choi should not become lost among the excitement of competition. Taekwondo, like all of the martial arts, is a system for training the mind and body, but with particular emphasis on the development of moral character. Students would not be able to perform impressive, high jump-kicks or break piles of bricks without first mastering their minds.

It takes great trust and belief to hit a wooden board with your bare fist, or to attempt to kick a target above your own height. Taekwondo is not an art for the faint-hearted or the weak-minded. But for those who can marry mind, body, and spirit into one cohesive entity, taekwondo will bring inner peace and assurance.

THE FIVE TENETS OF TAEKWONDO

When General Choi Hong Hi first formulated the martial art of taekwondo according to his moral beliefs, he based it on more than just physical training. It was training for both the mind and the spirit as well.

General Choi set out five tenets, or principles, by which taekwondo students should attempt to live their lives. These tenets were designed to help taekwondo students become better people and to help them make the world a better place. The five tenets are: courtesy (ye ui), integrity (yom chi), perseverance (in nee), self-control (guk gi), and indomitable spirit (baekjul boolgool).

COURTESY (YE UI)

Courtesy in taekwondo training means being polite and respectful to both your instructor and fellow pupils. Respect for your instructor is particularly important in taekwondo. He or she should be referred to as Sir, Miss, or Master. Your instructor will have reached his or her grade through many years of diligent training, so you should treat him or her with due respect.

You should also never question in public anything your instructor says. If you disagree with something he or she has said or done, wait until the end of the session and talk to him or her about it in private. You should also adhere to the taekwondo rules and etiquette at all times, both in the **dojang** (training hall) and out of it.

INTEGRITY (YOM CHI)

Integrity relates to having a conscience and knowing right from wrong. A taekwondo student should not practice the art for the wrong reasons. Taekwondo should be studied to make yourself a better person, to get fit, or for self-defense purposes—not to boost your ego or to be used to harm someone else. Students who want to learn taekwondo for reasons other than to improve themselves or to make the world a better place will quickly be discovered and banned from their club.

PERSEVERANCE (IN NEE)

A student of any martial art must persevere. You must be patient when learning a new art, technique, or skill. Many of the arts, techniques, and skills that you will learn will be difficult, and it will take many hours of practice just to become proficient—let alone an expert. You should always

It is only by observing and respecting the five tenets of taekwondo that a student can reach the pinnacle of this demanding sport and art, and dream of becoming an Olympic or world champion.

set goals for yourself and try to reach these goals throughout your training. You should also be aware, however, that the learning process lasts forever. You will never perfect any technique; no matter how high your grade is or how good you become, there will always be room for improvement. A dedicated taekwondo student will recognize this fact and always strive to better him- or herself.

SELF-CONTROL (GUK GI)

Because taekwondo is a physical martial art that involves lethal kicking and striking moves, you should always exercise self-control when practicing. During training, you should never try to hurt your partner. You should look after each other and try to work together so you can both improve your skills.

Training sometimes involves free sparring, which is essentially a form of free fighting. You must never lose control in such a situation, as your practice partner is also, likely, your friend. Even on the street, in a self-defense situation, you should always maintain self-control. Your aim is to protect yourself from injury, not to cause injury to your attacker.

INDOMITABLE SPIRIT (BAEKJUL BOOLGOOL)

The last tenet of taekwondo is that you should have an indomitable spirit. This means having a big heart, as well as the ability to tackle any situation, no matter how highly the odds are stacked against you. A student who acts against injustice regardless of the odds is said to have an indomitable spirit. This spirit comes from inside, from the energy force in the center of your body. You may be born with this spirit, but you can also develop it through training. The principle of indomitable spirit almost certainly stems from the principle to never retreat in battle, which was originated by the Buddhist monk Wong Kwang.

THE TAEKWONDO OATH

The taekwondo oath forms the student's book of rules. All students should learn it, as it is often recited at the beginning of a class, as well as at tournaments and functions. The oath states:

> *I shall observe the tenets of taekwondo.*
> *I shall respect my instructor and seniors.*
> *I shall never misuse taekwondo.*
> *I shall be a champion of freedom and justice.*
> *I shall build a more peaceful world.*

There are also five morals and 10 training codes set out in some taekwondo schools to remind students of their responsibilities. The five morals are: humanity, righteousness, **propriety**, wisdom, and trust. It is imperative that students practice these virtues to help build character in themselves and to better society.

The 10 training codes in some taekwondo schools relate to being a good student. A student becomes "good" by showing respect, having trust and faith in the instructor, setting a good example for his or her juniors, practicing meticulously to improve his or her skills, and by making sacrifices for the good of the club—or for the art itself. This means sacrificing your time to teach others and attending demonstrations and events. Not all clubs set out these morals and training codes.

The Elements of Taekwondo

There is a lot more to taekwondo than just putting some pads on and sparring with a friend. Every individual part of taekwondo was designed for a specific reason. Taekwondo is, after all, the result of many years of study by General Choi. The main elements of taekwondo that you should be aware of are stances, blocks, foot techniques, hand techniques, breaking, and patterns.

STANCES (SOGI)

Certain basic principles apply to all stances, known as **sogi**, such as standing with good posture, a straight back, and relaxed shoulders, but with a tensed torso. Your chin should be kept up, and you should be perfectly balanced, with good weight distribution between each leg.

ATTENTION STANCE (CHARYIOT SOGI)

The first stance you will learn is the attention stance. You should adopt this at the beginning of a class before bowing to your instructor. For the attention stance, your feet should be together, but facing out at about 45 degrees. Your fists should be clenched and your arms straight, just away from your sides.

Taekwondo is not just about kicking and punching. There are many elements to this martial art, such as stances or blocks, including this one, which uses both arms to guard from both a high and a front attack.

STANCES

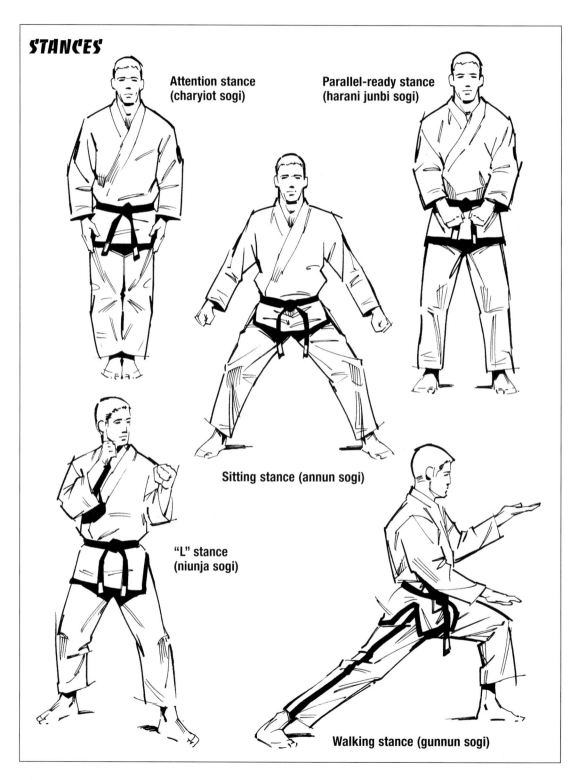

Attention stance
(charyiot sogi)

Parallel-ready stance
(harani junbi sogi)

Sitting stance (annun sogi)

"L" stance
(niunja sogi)

Walking stance (gunnun sogi)

PARALLEL-READY STANCE (NARANI JUNBI SOGI)

Your instructor will call out "charyiot," which means "attention." You will bow and then usually move into the parallel-ready stance. To reach this position, move your left foot out to the left until your feet are shoulder-width apart. Your hands come to the front of your body, with your fists clenched and elbows slightly bent. From this position, you will be ready to move quickly into any stance, whether on its own or in combination with a technique.

SITTING STANCE (ANNUN SOGI)

The sitting stance is used to practice punching. Move your left leg out until your feet are one and a half shoulder-widths apart. Your feet should be facing forwards. You literally "sit" into the stance—your knees are bent and pushed forwards, hanging over your toes. Your bottom is lowered, and your back should, as always, be straight.

You will usually move into this position while performing a punch. Although you can just remain in sitting stance, with your arms out to your sides, you will usually have one fist out in front of you, with the other on your hip, as if you were punching out.

WALKING STANCE (GUNNUN SOGI)

The walking stance is the most common stance for practicing techniques, as you can block, kick, punch, and strike from it with equal ease. From the parallel-ready stance, stride forwards with your left leg so that your foot lands one and a half shoulder-widths in front of your back foot. Your feet should not be directly in line with each other, however; they should remain in line with your shoulders. Your front knee should be bent so that your shin forms a vertical line from your ankle to your knee. Your back leg should be locked straight. Both feet should be facing forwards.

"L" STANCE (NIUNJA SOGI)

The "L" stance is used in some patterns and is commonly used to practice jabs, but its main purpose is in sparring. As the name suggests, in this stance, your feet form an "L" shape, with your back foot pointing out 90 degrees to the side and your front foot facing forwards. Whereas the other stances require equal weight distribution on both legs, in the "L" stance, about 60 to 70 percent of your weight should be over your back leg. This allows you to quickly transfer all your weight to your back leg and lift up your front leg to kick. Your hands should be held high out in front of you, ready to either punch or block.

During sparring, students usually bounce lightly in this stance so that they can move about quickly.

TRADITIONAL PATTERNS

Patterns are a sequence of moves and techniques that are performed in a natural and rhythmic way. They are an essential part of learning taekwondo. At each grading, you are required to perform at least one pattern, and they get longer and more complicated the higher your grade. Grand Master General Choi developed 24 patterns, each of which relates to a historical Korean figure.

The moves within a pattern follow a set structure. It is important to get the timing and accuracy of the moves right, because in a pattern, you should

Destruction is one element that sets Korean arts apart from Japanese arts. Taekwondo tournaments and demonstrations regularly feature gravity-defying feats of breaking, such as this one.

The initial method to learn how to break boards or bricks is to use a destruction "horse" which supports the boards you are trying to break. Gradually, over time, you can build up the number and density of boards you attempt to break.

begin and end in the same spot (this is not always easy when the pattern involves jumping). These patterns should be powerful. Your muscles should be tensed at the moment of impact for each technique.

Breath control is important throughout the performance of a pattern. You must learn to exhale on the point of impact for all techniques. This may seem a little embarrassing or silly at first, but it adds power and crispness to techniques, and in grading, you will be marked on breath control.

Many taekwondo patterns are

PATTERNS

Patterns form a vital part of taekwondo training and are usually practiced as a group to help everyone get the right timing.

traditional, but there are modern patterns as well. These modern patterns are called **sabang hyung** or pilsung, and differ from the traditional patterns in that the techniques do not end sharply; rather, they follow through freely into the next technique. These patterns supposedly offer more realistic moves for self-defense purposes.

GYOKPA: BREAKING OR DESTRUCTION

The destruction element of taekwondo sets it apart from many of the other martial arts. Every technique you learn (other than blocking techniques) can be used for breaking purposes.

GOOD BREAKING TECHNIQUE

It is important not to pick up bad habits when learning any technique, but this rule is especially true of breaking techniques. You may get away with an improper foot position for a kick during sparring or pad work; but when it comes to breaking, if your foot position is wrong, you could hurt yourself or face the embarrassment of struggling when other students are finding it easy. Good technique is vital for breaking, as is confidence.

Most taekwondo schools have specially made boards that fit together and break apart when hit with enough power on the join between them. Breaking can be daunting at first, and will usually hurt the first few times you attempt it. But part of your training is to have trust in your instructor, to persevere, and to have an indomitable spirit. Your instructor will not ask you to break something that will cause you injury (unless your technique fails you).

Your instructor may also test your character by giving you a board to break that should be beyond your capabilities to see whether you have the mental strength necessary to take on the challenge. If your technique is correct and your timing and speed are good, you may even surprise yourself by breaking something you did not expect to.

THE UNIFORM

The taekwondo uniform (called a **dobok**) is similar to that of most martial arts. It consists of a thin, white, open jacket and loose white pants. The

Balance is a vital element of taekwondo. A competitor must be on perfect balance to score with an attack. Although the athleticism in this picture is impressive, neither competitor manages to land a scoring blow, as neither is on balance.

Students only begin to practice destruction once they reach a certain level. The best exponents of taekwondo can attempt feats such as this, where the kicker is trying to stay in the air long enough to break two boards with two separate kicks.

jacket may have a zipper at the front; some modern uniforms have a special top that is pulled on, like a loose sweater. No matter which uniform your club uses, you will always have a belt tied around your waist. Unlike the Japanese arts, which only use white and black belts (and where Western countries have adopted colored belts to denote rank), taekwondo was designed to use colored belts.

In taekwondo, each belt color has been chosen for a specific reason, and each has a meaning behind it. The belt colors denote the practitioner's grade. There are 10 grades, or **kups**, before the black belt, but just five colored belts. Therefore, the higher grades within the same colored-belt level wear tags on their belts of the color of the next belt up to show that they are halfway between the two colored belts.

The kups run in descending order, so that 10th kup is the lowest grade and 1st kup is the highest, before the black belt. There are grades within the black belt as well, called dans. Dan grades run in ascending order, with the highest being the 9th dan, the grade of Grand Master General Choi Hong Hi.

BELT COLORS

In taekwondo, the meaning of the colored belts is as follows:

White: signifies the innocence of a beginner

Yellow: signifies the earth from which a plant sprouts and takes root, just as the foundations of taekwondo are laid

Green: signifies the growth of a plant, just as taekwondo skills begin to develop

Blue: signifies heaven or the sky, towards which a plant grows, just as taekwondo skills improve

Red: signifies the sun, energy, and the determination to study

Black: the opposite of white; it signifies maturity in taekwondo

These meanings were invented by Choi when he created taekwondo. Although the belts run in similar colored sequences to other arts, Choi picked his colors for specific reasons.

COMPETITION

As mentioned, there are two rival taekwondo ruling bodies. The most notable differences between them are reflected in their competition rules. The simple difference is that the WTF allows full-contact contests, whereas the ITF allows only semi-contact contests.

In full-contact contests, fighters wear head and chest guards, as the head and chest are the target areas for attack. Scores are awarded for successful kicks to the head or body, with one point scored for each successful blow. Punching to the head is banned, but you can score by punching to the body as long as the punch moves your opponent. It is difficult to knock an opponent back with a body punch through a chest guard, however, so punches rarely earn points. Full-contact contests tend to be completely dominated by kicks. This is the style in which taekwondo competitions are fought at the Olympics.

Semi-contact taekwondo uses foot, hand, shin, and head guards, but only allows semi-contact fighting. That means that you do not follow through with a technique; you must withdraw your foot or hand on impact. The rules differ slightly from full-contact taekwondo. Punches to the head are allowed in the semi-contact style because they do not use full force. A punch scores one point; a kick to the body scores two; a kick to head scores three; and a jump kick that lands on either the head or the body scores four points.

In both styles, the fighter with the highest score at the end of the contest is declared the winner (in full-contact taekwondo, you can also win by knocking your opponent out). Taekwondo uses weight categories to keep contests fair. There are usually only three or four different weight categories for both men and women. Being big and heavy is not necessarily an advantage, however. Fighters wear pads, thus equalizing the size factor, and smaller, lighter fighters

In the International Taekwondo Federation style, competitors cannot strike with full contact. This allows them to punch to the head, although the fighter on the left has put in an illegal low kick to the back of the knees.

tend to be quicker anyway. Penalties are awarded for infringements, such as grabbing your opponent's leg, low blows, and illegal strikes.

Whichever style your club is affiliated with will be clarified when you join, and your training will be geared towards those rules. Before you start sparring, you should make sure you are clear about the rules at your club. Fight durations vary (depending on the competition and your grade), so find these out before attending a competition. **Bouts** can last as little as one two-minute round, which means you have no time to pace yourself and must attack right at the beginning of the fight. In longer bouts, you may need to fight more tactically and possibly conserve energy early on so you can finish strongly.

Taekwondo Techniques

It has been said that the best form of defense is attack, but it is always handy to know some defense skills, too, just in case. The first and most important skill to be taught when you learn taekwondo is how to block (known as makgi). It is no good learning how to kick and punch your opponent if you cannot defend yourself from an attack.

BLOCKING TECHNIQUES

Whether you are practicing patterns, controlled sparring, or free sparring, you are always going to need to use blocks. You cannot rely on evasion to avoid blows in free sparring. Furthermore, patterns and controlled sparring require specific blocks at set times against predetermined moves.

For the purposes of this book, we will look at the most basic blocking moves that will allow you to defend yourself efficiently and effectively during sparring. These moves will be described in the manner in which they are performed in patterns. Once you get into a sparring scenario, however, you will have to rely on your wits and reactions to block a kick or punch. Whichever blocking technique you choose will be up to you—as long as you avoid being struck.

The techniques of taekwondo are split into three distinctive categories: blocks, hand strikes, and kicks. The fundamental emphasis in taekwondo is on kicking, as the legs are the most powerful attack weapons.

Before learning how to strike an opponent, students must first learn to defend themselves. Therefore, the first techniques a student will be taught are the blocking techniques, such as this double low-forearm block.

THE REACTION ARM

Whenever you perform a block, it should be done with a quick, sharp movement and should end suddenly, with a snap. While your blocking arm is in action, your other arm must move in the opposite direction with equal power—this is called the "reaction" arm. The reaction arm is based on the principle of physics whereby every action has an equal and opposite reaction. You must always have a reaction arm, as this gives more power to the block.

LOW-SECTION BLOCK (NAJUNDE MAKGI)

The low-section block is a typical defense to a low, rising front kick aimed either at the groin or the stomach. It is practiced in the walking stance, with your left leg forward. Clench your fists and bring your hands up to your right shoulder, twisting slightly to the right as you do so. Cross your hands, with your right hand over your left. As you twist back to a square stance, bring your left hand down sharply, just over your left knee. Keep your arm slightly bent as you finish the block, and keep your knuckles facing away from you. At the same time that you bring down your blocking arm, bring your right hand down to your hip. Your clenched fist should be just touching your hip, with your elbow bent out behind you. The block works in exactly the same way on the other side, although this time, you cross your hands left over right.

INNER FOREARM BLOCK (AN PALMOK MAKGI)

During a taekwondo contest, fighters stand side-on to their opponents to

LOWER-SECTION BLOCK

STEP 1: The blocking arm begins high up to the blocker's ear as the attacker raises his knee for a roundhouse kick.

STEP 2: The blocking arm is thrust out in front of the blocker to meet the kick before it reaches her body.

try to reduce the area they have to aim at. If a fighter were to stand squarely in front of his or her opponent, it would be much harder to defend him- or herself, as he or she would be opening up his or her whole torso to an attack.

From a side-on stance, a fighter only shows the side of his or her body to the opponent and can easily guard that area with his or her leading arm. Consequently, the most common attacks are done with turning kicks, as fighters try to get around the side and attack their opponent's torso. These turning kicks usually attack the middle or high sections of the torso, which can be defended with both inner and outer forearm blocks.

The inner forearm block is done with the part of your forearm that runs in a straight line from your thumb to your elbow joint. Any block that uses this part of your arm is called an inner forearm block, regardless of what direction the attack is coming from or in what direction you block. If you hold up your left arm and twist your fist so that your knuckles face away from you, this inner forearm block would be used to block an attack from your left.

The blocking movement starts from your hips, which twist to the right. Bring your blocking arm up in a circular motion to block a middle-section blow with the same snapping action as in the other blocks, making sure to twist your wrist so that your knuckles face forwards. Your elbow should be bent, with your arm out in front of you. As always, your reaction hand finishes on your hip.

When sparring, you generally use your leading arm to block, so you should block to your outside. If you try to block the punch across your own body, your inside, the punch would probably glance off your blocking arm and possibly still hit you. You would also leave yourself open to be struck by a follow-up punch from your opponent's other hand. By blocking your opponent's punch across his or her body, you can now follow up with a counterpunch of your own.

The inner forearm block is more limited than the outer forearm block (see the following section), as you can only really use it to block to your outside. To use it to block to your inside, you would have to turn your wrist so that your knuckles face towards you, and then swing the block across your own body.

In this movement, your inner forearm naturally starts twisting towards you, which would stop you from using the inner forearm to block a blow coming at you.

OUTER FOREARM BLOCK (BAKAT PALMOK MAKGI)

The outer forearm block can be used as a substitute for the inner forearm block. It is more versatile than the inner forearm block, as you can use it to block on either your inside or your outside. This block uses the part of your arm that runs in a straight line from your little finger to your elbow joint. You can turn your fist away from you to block to your inside, or turn it towards you to block to your outside.

The position this block starts from depends on whether you are blocking to your outside or to your inside. To block to your outside, start with your hands held up by your shoulder, with your wrists crossed over. To block to your inside, however, there is no traditional starting form. This is because you cannot cross your arms over, as then they would both have to travel in the same direction as you perform the block (this would cancel out the

INNER FOREARM BLOCK

STEP 1: The blocking arm begins underneath the reaction arm as the attacker lines up a jab.

STEP 2: The inner part of the forearm makes contact with the attacker's arm and deflects it away from the defender's body.

OUTER FOREARM, RISING, AND UPPER FOREARM BLOCKS

ABOVE: The outer forearm block uses an inward motion to deflect a blow across the open side of the body.

ABOVE RIGHT: The rising block uses the outer section of the forearm to stop any blows coming down onto the defender's head.

RIGHT: The upper forearm block is the most common block in sparring and can be used against almost any low- or mid-section kick.

principle of every action having an equal and opposite reaction). Just swing your blocking arm across your body to deflect the blow.

Just like the example in the inner forearm block, the defender blocks the attacker's striking arm across his or her body so he or she cannot follow up with a punch with his or her other hand. By contrast, the defender is now perfectly placed to counterattack with a head punch of his or her own over his or her opponent's attacking arm.

RISING BLOCK (CHOOKYO MAKGI)

The rising block protects your head from a high attack coming down on top of it. In a taekwondo contest, the attack could either come from an ax kick or from a jumping-back fist. In a self-defense context, however, the attack is most likely to be from a stick, pipe, or weapon of some sort being brought down on your head.

Perform this block in the walking stance. Bring your hands up to your shoulder, and twist in the same way as for the low-section block. From there, however, your blocking arm is raised upwards. Where the block ends, your arm should make a perfect right angle. Your arm should be vertical from your shoulder to your elbow and horizontal from your elbow to your fist. Your fist should be clenched, with your palm facing forwards. Your forearm is the blocking tool.

In a self-defense situation, you will likely be blocking a weapon being brought down on the top of your head. Therefore, your forearm should be high enough and forward enough to stop the weapon from hitting your head. It should be above the level of your forehead and a few inches out in front of you. Your reaction arm will come to rest on your hip.

BLOCKING STANCE AND FINISHING POSITION

In taekwondo, you will always spar with one foot in front of the other. When sparring, you would not block while in a walking stance; it is more likely that you would be in a stance resembling the "L" stance. Your block should always finish over your forward knee.

UPPER FOREARM BLOCK (PALMOK MAKGI)

There is no specific Korean term to describe the upper forearm, so this block is simply referred to as a "forearm block." The upper forearm runs from the back of your hand to your elbow joint. It is not a sharp ridge, like the inner and outer forearms; it is a flatter surface. You would use this block most often in sparring to block a low-section kick, usually as you are moving away from your opponent to evade a kick.

The idea behind the upper forearm block is to deflect your opponent's leg away from you as you try to evade a kick. As you are using the flat part of your forearm rather than a ridged part, this block will be less harmful to your opponent's shin. It is often used in semi-free sparring or in three-step sparring, where you and your partner are working together as a pair.

Often, the upper forearm block is the swiftest defensive measure. When sparring, you keep your arms high in order to block any attack to your middle or high sections, but it is quick and easy to drop your forearm below your elbow to block a low kick. For this block, you should keep your hand open and relaxed.

KICKING TECHNIQUES

Taekwondo consists of roughly 70 percent kicking techniques and 30 percent hand techniques. Therefore, greater emphasis is placed on kicks than on punching or striking. This bias towards kicking techniques results in some spectacular demonstrations involving flying jump-kicks to break boards, sometimes held up by a person sitting on another person's shoulders.

Your average taekwondo student, however, cannot perform such gravity-defying feats and has to content him- or herself with the basic kicks. That in itself is no minor challenge, however, as there is a lot more to kicking than just aiming the top of your foot at your opponent. You have to know which foot part to strike with for each different technique. The main foot parts used in kicking are the ball, the heel, and the foot sword (the outer ridge). With each kick, it is important to strike with the right part of the foot to get maximum power behind it.

There are a few basic principles that all effective kicks depend upon. One of these is to always lean forward as you kick. By leaning over your kick, you put all

The main focus in taekwondo is on the kicking techniques. To kick effectively, a student needs to have good balance, suppleness, and technique, all of which are evident in this high-section side kick.

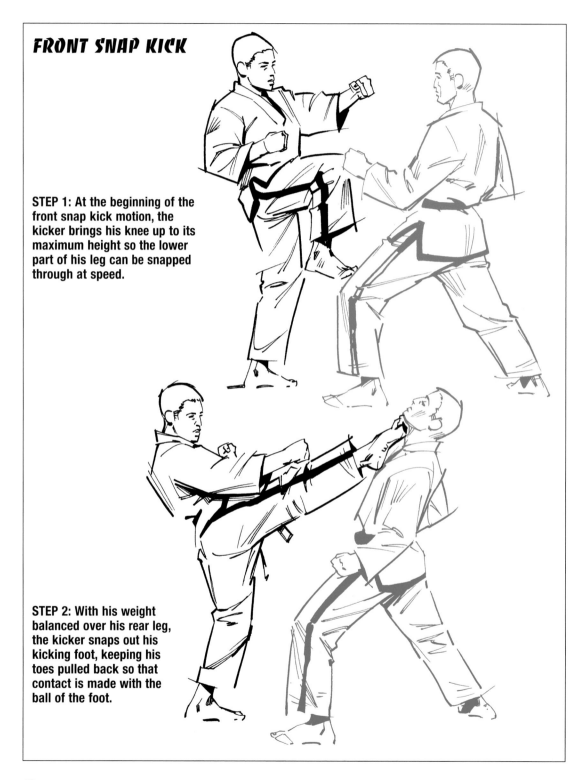

FRONT SNAP KICK

STEP 1: At the beginning of the front snap kick motion, the kicker brings his knee up to its maximum height so the lower part of his leg can be snapped through at speed.

STEP 2: With his weight balanced over his rear leg, the kicker snaps out his kicking foot, keeping his toes pulled back so that contact is made with the ball of the foot.

your weight into it. If you lean backwards, you will not be able to generate any power, and will probably get knocked backwards. You should also keep your kicking leg relaxed until the moment of impact, at which point it should be fully extended.

You should use the knee of your standing leg to get extra spring and power into your kicks. You do this by bending it and then straightening on impact, staying well balanced throughout the motion. Last, it is vital that you withdraw your kicking leg quickly after impact. This is done both to stop your opponent from grabbing it and to allow you to follow up the kick with another technique.

FRONT SNAP KICK (AP CHA BUSIGI)

The front snap kick is the simplest kick. It is a straight, forward-pointing kick that can be aimed at either the middle or high sections. You can perform a front snap kick using either the front leg or the rear leg. Obviously, it will be quicker using the front leg, but it will be more powerful off the rear leg, because you will have put more momentum into it. When kicking with your rear leg, you should leave just enough distance between yourself and your opponent to be closed down when you lunge forward.

When sparring, most of your weight should be on your back leg. Therefore, to kick with your front leg, you just have to lift it up; but to kick with your back leg, you must first shift your weight onto your front foot, which takes more time. Whichever foot you kick with, you will have to bring your knee up high to begin with before flicking out your lower leg. If you do not lift your knee up high first, the kick will have less speed and power.

The front snap kick strikes using the ball of the foot, so make sure you keep your toes pointing upwards on impact and stretch the ball of your foot out in front of your heel. Always keep your guard up throughout the kick, and use the spring in your standing knee to generate extra power. In competitions, the front snap kick is primarily a speed kick that scores a quick point, but it is difficult to connect, as the only part of your opponent to aim for (they are standing side-on) is usually his or her lower ribcage, just beneath his or her guard.

SIDE-PIERCING KICK (YOP CHA JIRUGI)

The side-piercing kick is another straight kick that would also be aimed at either the area below your opponent's guard or at his or her head, if you can kick to the high section. For breaking purposes, you would use your rear leg for a side-piercing kick, as you can generate more power that way. For sparring purposes, however, you would always use the front leg, as there simply is not enough time to use the rear leg—there is just too much distance for your foot to cover to stand any chance of landing a kick.

From the "L" stance, raise your front knee to waist height before jabbing out your foot. Your knee should be at the height you want to kick, or as near to it as possible, before you begin the kicking action. As you jab your foot out, you should pivot on the ball of your standing foot until your heel is almost facing your opponent. This will allow you to keep your weight over your leg and to turn your ankle inwards so that you strike with the foot sword rather than the foot sole.

It is important to strike with the foot sword rather than the sole in order for the kick to be effective. The smaller the area of your foot that makes

SIDE-PIERCING KICK

STEP 1: The attacker brings her knee up to its maximum height and swivels on the ball of her standing foot so her hip is fully turned before beginning the kicking action.

STEP 2: As there is no need to turn any further, she strikes out with her foot sword in a straight line to her target. This gives maximum speed and power to her kick.

contact with your opponent, the more concentrated your weight and power will be over that area. It is the same as the difference between hitting someone with the ridge of your hand and an open palm. The open palm may make more of a slapping sound, but it is not as powerful as the thin ridge of your hand, which will do a lot more damage.

TURNING KICK (DOLLYO CHAGI)

The turning kick is one of the most common attacks in taekwondo competition and sparring. The leading leg is the preferred attacking leg, but the rear leg is often used for this type of kick, as you take a step back to fend off an opponent who is moving towards you.

The turning kick is used to attack your opponent's torso from the side when you have little to aim at with a straight kick. It is illegal to kick an opponent in the back, so if one fighter is standing with his or her left side forward, and the other with his or her right side forward, neither fighter can score with a turning kick to the torso with their leading leg. In this instance, you could attempt to score with your rear leg, although this is usually done as part of a combination of kicks rather than a single attack.

As with most kicks, you need to lift your knee up quite high for the turning kick. This also serves to help disguise the direction of your kick. With your knee lifted high, you can kick either to the high section or the middle section of your opponent's body with equal ease. Your knee should be lifted slightly to the side so that you can get the rotation movement necessary to come around your opponent's front blocking arm and strike his or her front torso. You should pivot on the ball of your standing foot as you execute the kick, but do not turn as far as you would for the side kick (see

TURNING KICK

STEP 1: For the turning kick, the kicker should be balanced on the ball of her standing foot so she can easily pivot her hips. The knee is brought up quickly so that it has minimum distance to travel through the kick.

STEP 2: With a slight pivot on her standing foot, the kicker keeps her weight balanced over her standing leg as she swings the lower part of her kicking leg at its target, connecting with the ball of her foot.

BACK KICK

STEP 1: To perform the back kick, the kicker spins her head and upper torso around as she lifts her kicking leg, so that she can see her opponent before kicking.

STEP 2: Still with her back largely turned towards her opponent, the kicker thrusts out her foot similarly to the side kick, continuing to rotate her torso throughout the motion.

the previous section). In fact, you only need to pivot until your heel is at an angle of about 45 degrees to your opponent.

The turning kick uses the ball of the foot (you get more power from this part). In sparring, however, you would usually use the top of your foot, as this area is padded. The reason for this is that in taekwondo competitions, you score points as in amateur boxing: simply by striking your opponent in a scoring area. You do not get any extra points for power, and so you should connect with the top of your foot. For breaking, however, you need that extra power, so you would use the ball of your foot (if you kicked a board with the top of your foot, you would either break or severely bruise your foot).

BACK-PIERCING KICK (DWIT CHA JIRUGI)

A vital aspect of sparring in any martial art is to always keep looking at your opponent so you will be ready to react to anything he or she does. This is why the back kick is a risky one: for a split second, you have to turn your back to your opponent. Although you take your chances when using this kick, if it works, it can be devastatingly powerful.

The back kick tends to be a defensive kick, and is performed as your opponent moves towards you. While your opponent is moving forwards, he or she cannot launch a kick, thus allowing you the time you need to turn your back and strike out with a back kick. If your opponent is standing still, however, and you are moving forwards, you should not attempt a back kick, as he or she will have too much time to counter it.

The execution of the back-piercing kick is similar to that of the side kick. To begin, lift your back foot up off the mat and turn your head and shoulders backwards. As you start to turn your head and shoulders, begin

AX KICK

STEP 1: In the initial motion for this, the kicker brings her foot up as high as she can above her opponent's head.

STEP 2: Keeping her knee locked throughout, the kicker brings her heel or the ball of her foot down at speed on top of her opponent.

pivoting on your front foot. Do not start the kicking motion until you have turned your head all the way around and you can see your opponent again. When you can, jab out your leg in the same way as you would for a side kick: in a straight line, making contact with the foot sword.

With this kick, the spinning motion generates extra speed, which in turn increases the power on impact. You should always lead the turning action with your head and shoulders, letting your hips follow. Another advantage to the back kick is disguise. As you turn your back and start to bring up your rear leg, your opponent cannot see your kicking leg for a split second. As you bring it around, your opponent might think that you are attempting a reverse-hooking kick or a reverse-turning kick. Thus, your opponent does not know what to expect. The back kick is not one to try repeatedly, however, as its effectiveness relies a great deal on the element of surprise.

AX KICK (NAERO CHAGI)

The ax kick is effective, both as an attacking move and as a defensive move. It is quite a simple kick, but it requires great flexibility in the groin and the hamstring of the kicking leg. To perform an ax kick, bring your leg straight up and drop it straight down on your opponent, aiming usually for his or her collarbone or nose. If you were to use an ax kick in a self-defense situation or to break bricks, you would use the back of your heel as the impact tool. For sparring and competition purposes, however, you should use the sole of your foot, as this will give you that little bit of extra reach. Keep your knee locked throughout the technique, or the kick will lose its power and precision.

The ax kick is a difficult one to do with your leading leg, because you need to swing it in order to develop sufficient momentum to get the height you need. It can be done using the front or leading leg, but you need to do a little skip into it with your back leg in order to get some momentum into your swing.

The ax kick is not a fast kick—you would not use it for a quick strike. It is a powerful kick that is usually followed up by other techniques. It is better

A jump kick is a difficult skill to master, but looks impressive once it is pulled off. Even though the student is in the air here, the same principles of weight distribution and balance apply.

JUMP KICK

STEP 1: The kicker leaps into the air, leading with his reaction leg and keeping his kicking leg back.

STEP 2: At the point of maximum elevation, the kicker thrusts his kicking leg straight forwards and his reaction leg backwards, keeping his momentum going forward throughout the kick.

KICKING TO THE HIGH SECTION

Kicking to the high section of the body can be tricky for a number of reasons. First of all, it requires a lot of flexibility in your groin. It is also difficult to kick high while remaining balanced. Furthermore, people often overcompensate with their upper body when trying to kick high and end up leaning back a lot to get their foot high enough. This results in a substantial loss of power and renders the kick fairly ineffectual.

to use the rear leg when performing this kick. That way, you can attack from a greater distance from your opponent. As you begin the kick, the position of your leading foot will become the position of your back foot by the time you make contact with your opponent (this makes for a lot of distance for your foot to cover). This is a difficult kick to block or defend against; evasion is usually the only form of defense against it.

JUMP KICK (TWIGY CHAGI)

Jump kicks are what make taekwondo such a spectacular sport to watch. In demonstrations, experts produce some outrageous high kicks. These extravagant moves are rarely seen in competition, but there is another place for jump kicks in taekwondo: they can be effective weapons.

In the jump phase of the kick, you can cover greater distances than you could with a standing kick. You can use your weight and momentum to get a lot of power into the kick. There is also the advantage of your angle of attack. To kick to the high section of your opponent's body with a standing kick, you will invariably have to kick upwards, which will lose both speed and power; but from a jump kick, you can reach the high section with a straight kick, and therefore not lose any power.

The straightforward jump kick uses a scissor motion done with the legs. This motion can confuse opponents, who will be unsure which leg you are attacking with.

Starting from the "L" stance, bend your knees and jump high into the air as you step forward with your rear leg. You should use the stepping motion of your rear leg to help get the spring you need to jump up. At the peak of your jump, bring your kicking leg through with the same motion as you would for the front snap kick. You can also kick with your rear leg (you would usually only use this leg if you were backing away from your opponent). Jump into the air as you take a step backwards with your leading leg, and kick out with your rear leg as your opponent is moving towards you.

This is the most simple of the jump kicks, but there are many others that you can learn. In fact, almost any kick you learn in taekwondo can be transformed into a jump kick simply by jumping as you do it. Some are more effective than others, however. Some are primarily demonstration techniques, such as the jump side-kick, which makes for an exuberant breaking demonstration, but is impractical in competition.

STRIKING AND PUNCHING TECHNIQUES

Although taekwondo is a predominantly kick-oriented martial art, there is still a wide array of punching techniques (called **jirugi**) and striking techniques (called **taerigi**). Depending on which taekwondo style you practice, punches and strikes take on different levels of importance. But whichever style you choose, you must learn hand techniques for close-in contact fighting. In this type of fighting, you may not have enough space to swing a kick at an opponent, but you may be able to get a punch in.

In the WTF style, you can only punch to your opponent's chest pad, and you can only score if you knock him or her backwards with that punch. Punches rarely carry enough power to knock someone backwards, however, especially through a chest pad, so WTF-style competitions are completely dominated by kicking.

The ITF style, which is semi-contact, allows scoring punches to both the head and body. In this style, however, the scoring system still favors kicks over punches. The score for a punch is just one point, compared with two points for a body kick, three for a kick to the head, and four for a jump kick. Therefore, fighters in the ITF style are more inclined to use punches and hand techniques than those in the WTF style, but kicks are still the preferred method of attack.

Although many people take up taekwondo competitively, there are also many people who enjoy it simply as a form of self-defense or to keep fit. Regardless of which style you study, it is important to learn hand techniques, as they could prove useful in a self-defense situation on the street. You also need to perform hand techniques at grading, in patterns, and when breaking.

Hand techniques involve a lot more than just punches. Other than the knuckles, there are four parts of the hand used to strike blows to an opponent; the fingertips, the palm, and both ridges of your hand can all be used to deliver a strike. Punches tend to be the preferred hand technique in

Punching and striking techniques may not be used in competition as much as kicks, but they form an integral part of patterns. To punch or strike effectively, a student must also observe the principles of balance and reaction.

REVERSE PUNCH

The reverse punch is executed with the opposite fist to the leading foot. Notice also how the reaction arm is brought back onto the student's hip.

competition, but you still need to learn each type of strike in order to become a proficient student of taekwondo. This section will cover six basic types of striking techniques using different parts of your hand.

THE STRIKE WEAPONS

Like the feet, most areas of the hands can be used as attack weapons—even the fingers. There are two main types of area to strike with—soft fleshy parts, like the palm; and hard bony parts, for example, the side of the forefinger knuckle. Whichever part of the hand is used, it is the target areas that cause the real danger in hand strikes. These are purely self-defense weapons and are designed to be aimed at the most vulnerable points on an attacker's body. Accordingly, they should never be used in competition or in sparring situations.

REVERSE PUNCH (SO BANDAE JIRUGI)

The reverse punch is really a demonstration punch used in patterns or for breaking, but it is generally the first punch a student is taught. A reverse punch is simply a straight, forward-direction punch, using the arm opposite to your leading leg. It is always done from a walking stance.

From a walking stance, stand with your arm (the one on the same side as your leading leg) straight out in front of you, with your fist clenched. Your other fist should be tucked in on your hip. From this position, bring your rear fist forwards to punch, and pull your leading fist back to your hip as the reaction to your punch.

As you bring your fist through from your hip, turn your wrist so that the back of your hand finishes facing upwards (rather than downwards, as at the starting position). Do not twist it until right at the end of the punch. Keep your arms relaxed until the moment of impact. You should make contact with your first two knuckles, as these are the strongest.

You would not use the reverse punch in competition, but it is good for learning how to punch and how to generate power from a punch. To get extra power, you have to put your hip into a punch. This means that when you begin to move your punching arm, you twist your hip backwards slightly, going forwards into the punch at the moment of impact.

In competition, fighters use jabs, hooks, and uppercuts, just like in boxing. The reverse punch teaches you the fundamentals of these types (and many other types) of punches. Each of these punches uses the same two knuckles on impact and the same twist of the hip to generate power as the reverse punch.

BACK FIST (DUNG JOOMUK)

The back fist strike is a common competition technique because it can be flicked out quickly and accurately in close combat. You can also squeeze a back fist strike through tight openings. By bending your elbow, you can attack using this strike from almost any angle.

The back fist strike should be practiced in the walking stance. It starts from a high crossover position by your opposite shoulder to your leading leg. Now bring your fist across your body in a circular motion until it is level with your shoulder. You should strike parallel to your own shoulder and bend your wrist outwards on impact, so your first two knuckles make contact with your target. As always, your reaction arm should be brought down to your hip, arriving just as your punching fist hits its target. You should also twist your hips slightly away from your target, and then back into it on impact.

BACK FIST

The back fist is like a short, sharp jab, aimed at the side of an opponent's head, and usually used as a quick-fire counterattack.

PALM-HEEL STRIKE (PYON JOOMUK TAERIGI)

The palm-heel strike is just like a straight punch, only executed with an open hand. For this strike, use the same movement as in the reverse punch, but keep your hand open and bend your wrist backwards on impact. The

PALM-HEEL STRIKE

The palm-heel strike uses the same movement as a reverse punch, except the attacker keeps her palm open and forward-facing, striking with the fleshy part at the bottom of her palm.

palm-heel strike can be performed with an open hand, with your fingers closed together, or with your fingers bent over.

The palm-heel strike is used for striking high body sections; it is almost always aimed at your opponent's nose, or under his or her chin. Contact is made with the lower part of your palm, just above the wrist and below the thumb. This can be a devastating blow, and so it is practiced only for self-defense purposes. These blows are not permitted in sparring, as a palm-heel strike that hits someone in the nose in an upward direction is dangerous and could cause a serious injury.

KNIFE-HAND STRIKE

The knife-hand strike uses the fleshy outside edge of the hand to strike and is usually aimed at an opponent's head.

The palm-heel strike is used primarily in breaking, but it still uses the same principles as other strikes. As you strike through with your arm, you should point your fingers at the target, pulling them back only at the last moment to make contact with the heel of the palm.

KNIFE-HAND STRIKE (SONKAL TAERIGI)

Knife-hand strikes are, like palm-heel strikes (see previous section), more prevalent as self-defense tools than as sparring weapons. A knife-hand strike would usually be aimed at an attacker's neck, which is not something you would attempt in sparring, and is illegal in competition.

The contact point for a knife-hand strike is the muscle that runs from your little finger to your wrist. This is a soft, thick muscle, which allows you to strike hard without hurting yourself. The knife-hand strike begins at shoulder level, with your striking palm twisted to face

A TWIST OF THE WRIST

The reason taekwondo punches use a twist of the wrist on impact is to ensure that you remain relaxed throughout the punch and only tense on impact. It is important to maintain maximum speed throughout a punch, and tensing too soon will slow it down. If you stick to these basic principles, you will quickly find that you can punch harder than you had expected, and you will soon be ready to attempt breaking with your hands.

away from you and your knuckles pointing towards you. Your fingertips should be curled in slightly, with your fingers and thumb all closed up tightly to reduce damage to your own hand.

You can practice the knife-hand strike while in a walking stance. Strike by making an arc movement initially away from you, and then cutting back across your body to strike directly out in front of you. Just before the moment of impact, twist your wrist so that your palm is facing upwards. This is a snapping technique, which means that you withdraw your hand immediately after impact rather than driving it through your opponent. The hip movement and reaction arm work in the same way as with all other strikes, and your arm should remain slightly bent on impact.

REVERSE KNIFE-HAND STRIKE (SONKAL DUNG TAERIGI)

The reverse knife-hand strike works in much the same way as the knife-hand strike, but with this strike, you use the opposite side of your hand:

the ridge that runs from your forefinger to your wrist. Also, with this strike, you actually strike with the side of your forefinger knuckle. Your fingertips should be curled over in the same way as with the knife-hand strike, but your thumb must be tucked into the palm of your hand so that it does not get in the way of the impact knuckle.

REVERSE KNIFE-HAND STRIKE

The reverse knife-hand strike uses the bony part of the hand running down from the forefinger and is usually aimed at the high section.

73

The reverse knife-hand strike uses a bigger arc than the knife-hand strike, as it is a less-natural movement for your arm and more room is needed to gather the momentum necessary to execute an effective strike. Your striking arm should begin across your body and then swing in an arc outwards and away from you, before coming back in to make contact with the side of your opponent's head or his or her face.

This technique can be used in sparring. It is usually used in a situation in which an opponent is going past you and you are turning your body to face him or her. The arm swing would be a natural extension of your turning body, and you could deliver a quick blow to the side of the head. In a self-defense situation, you would aim the strike at your attacker's face as you step slightly to the side of him or her to give yourself enough room to land the blow with an almost fully straightened arm.

FINGERTIP THRUST (SONKUP TAERIGI)

The fingertip thrust moves in the same manner as a reverse punch, but with the finger shape of the knife-hand strike. It is a straight blow, and is usually aimed at the solar plexus or neck. It is not allowed in sparring, as it is a dangerous blow. When executing this technique, your fingertips should be curled slightly inwards. The blow comes from the hip, like the reverse punch.

A fingertip thrust can be performed with either your knuckles facing outwards or upwards, but to get maximum snap and power, you must twist your wrist on impact. Your fingers need to be conditioned over a long period of time to become tough enough to perform an effective fingertip thrust.

FINGERTIP THRUST

The fingertip thrust is similar to the reverse punch, but the fingertips are used as the striking tool. It is important to keep them slightly bent so you do not break your fingers.

This conditioning can be tough and painful. People have been known to practice this move by thrusting their fingers into bags of beans or rice to toughen up the fingers.

As a self-defense weapon, the fingertip thrust is difficult to block, as you cup your fingers into a small area that can slip through narrow gaps. Note that this move can be deadly, however, and so you should use it only as a last resort.

Taekwondo Training

Taekwondo is about speed and power, and so most of the training focuses on one of these aspects. As it is largely a kicking-based art, with many high and spectacular kicks, taekwondo students also need to train their bodies to be able to perform high kicks. This means that a lot of groin-stretching exercises are needed.

Like any martial art or sport, it is important to warm up properly before exercising. In taekwondo, particular emphasis falls on the leg muscles, especially the groin area. Anyone who has attended an exercise class at school or college will know a little bit about stretching exercises and warming up, but it is important to apply some structure to your routine, such as starting at your neck and working your way down your body.

Taekwondo classes often begin with some jogging, push-ups, and sit-ups to get your muscles nice and warm, but the main exercise involves loosening up the groin. Students usually do a lot of straight-leg raises, which is the beginning movement of the ax kick. Swing your rear leg forwards and as high as possible before returning it to its starting position. Keep your leg straight throughout the movement, and try to edge it a bit higher with each swing.

Diligent practice is needed to attain high levels in taekwondo. This student will have spent a lot of painful hours stretching her groin to get the suppleness to be able to kick above her own head height.

STRETCHING

In taekwondo, you need a supple groin to enable you to kick to your opponent's head with speed and control. Most people can get their leg reasonably high by leaning over backwards as they swing it up, but this is the wrong movement; not only will you lose your balance, but you will also have no chance of scoring, since you cannot see your opponent. A supple groin will allow you to keep your head and torso leaning forward as you attempt a high kick so that you can remain focused on your opponent.

There are many ways to improve the flexibility in your groin, most of which require the help of a partner. One good exercise involves standing facing your partner. Lift your foot up to his or her shoulder, keeping both legs straight. Your partner then forces your foot up as high as possible until you start to feel pain. He or she should stop then and just hold your leg in that position for about a minute. Do the same exercise with your other leg. When you return back to the first leg, try to go a little bit higher than before. Regular repetition of this exercise will quickly improve your flexibility and ability to kick high.

This exercise can also help to increase your sideways flexibility. When you have your foot up on your partner's shoulder, stretch sideways (with your standing foot at 90 degrees to your partner) as well as forwards (with your standing foot facing your partner). This exercise will help stretch your hamstrings. The hamstrings need to be stretched thoroughly, as they are quite vulnerable to tears or strains with sudden ax kicks.

SPEED AND POWER TRAINING

Taekwondo students need strong legs—thighs in particular—for all the kicking they do in competition. The stances you practice will naturally

The importance of stretching can be seen here, where the fighter on the left has used greater suppleness to kick over her opponent's own kick and score with a head blow.

A GROIN-STRETCHING EXERCISE

Here is another exercise to try with a partner. Both of you should sit down, facing each other, with your legs stretched out as wide as possible in front of you. Have your partner put his or her feet on the insides of your ankles, and then have him or her push your feet out wider using his or her own feet. Your partner can do this by holding onto your belt and pulling you in towards him or her. As your partner pulls your groin in closer, his or her feet will naturally push your legs out wider, thus stretching your groin. Do this stretch until you start to feel pain, and then hold it there. As it becomes a little more comfortable, get your partner to pull you in a little bit closer still. Improving the flexibility in your groin takes a lot of time and should not be rushed. Make sure you ease it out gently, and never overdo it. Pain is your body's way of telling you to stop what you are doing, so listen to it.

build up your thigh muscles, but here is another exercise you could try. Put your back against a wall and slide down the wall until your legs form a right angle—as if you were sitting in a chair. Push your back against the wall to keep yourself from falling down on your bottom. Hold this position for about 30 seconds to a minute—whatever you can manage. Each time you do this exercise, try to beat your previous record. Only by competing against yourself will you improve. Eventually, you will find that you can sit against a wall for as long as you want without any problem.

Most training can be done within the routine of a club. Pad work (punching or kicking against a pad) is particularly good for improving both speed and power, and can be done with a partner. Whether punching or kicking a pad, you should always work on either your speed or your power.

To work on your speed, strike the pad as fast as you can, but always return to your starting position after each blow. For example, if practicing a turning kick with the reverse leg, after kicking the pad, return your kicking leg back behind your standing leg, reverting into the original stance you began with (probably an "L" stance in this case). Then kick again. Do high repetitions of between 20 and 50 kicks with each leg. You do not have to

FOCUS PAD WORK

Small focus pads can be used to improve the accuracy of kicking. Here, the man holds out the focus pad as the woman kicks it at full power. These can be used for any kicking or punching techniques.

kick with full power, as you are working to improve your speed, but you do need to kick as fast as possible.

For power training, do fewer repetitions, but concentrate harder on technique, and try to kick or punch using all of your power. See if you can move your partner with each blow. Make sure you are kicking or punching with the right part of the foot or hand, as technique is vital for power (as are

Sparring is an important part of taekwondo training. In semi-free or step-sparring, students may only wear hand and foot protectors, as they are not kicking or punching with full power.

PADDING EQUIPMENT

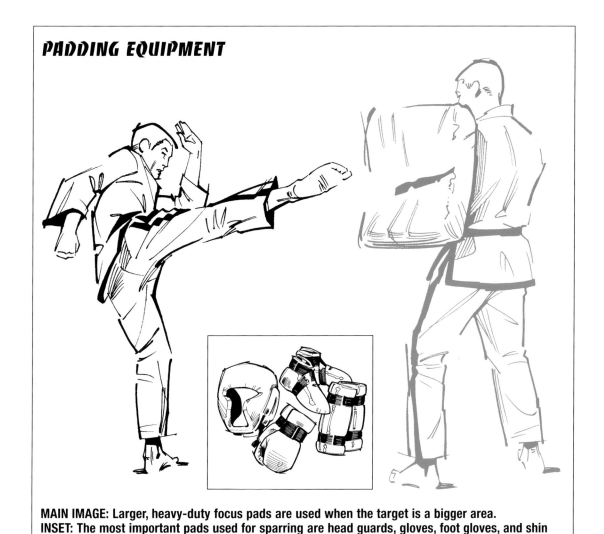

MAIN IMAGE: Larger, heavy-duty focus pads are used when the target is a bigger area.
INSET: The most important pads used for sparring are head guards, gloves, foot gloves, and shin pads (shown here). These are worn both for your own protection and your partner's.

speed and timing). You should also make sure that you put your hip into the technique and that you lean into your kicks.

CONDITIONING YOUR BODY

Taekwondo is not just about striking your opponent; you also have to be able to take a blow yourself. If your body is not hard and finely toned, your opponent's blows may hurt. You need to be in physically good shape to practice taekwondo. That does not mean as muscular as a body builder or as fit as a marathon runner, but somewhere in between. Push-ups will tone and strengthen your arms and chest if you do them with your hands wide apart, and sit-ups will work your stomach muscles. You should get used to doing high repetitions of both to tone your body above the waist.

Gym work can also help condition your body, but again, you must do the right kind of exercises. Men tend to like having big, bulky biceps, but that will not help your taekwondo skills. When going to the gym, you should do a balanced workout, concentrating on your whole body. Doing high repetitions with low weights will help increase strength slowly while also improving **anaerobic** stamina.

SPARRING

The most important part of your training is sparring. This is where you put on pads and have a semi-contact contest with a partner. There are three different types of sparring. Step sparring is where you have prearranged attacks and defenses, and you work together so that the moves flow smoothly. These are specifically designed as realistic combination attacks. One person puts the attacks together, while the other blocks them. This technique is also useful for the defender, as he or she has the opportunity to get used to fending off multiple attacks without the worry of actually being caught.

Semi-free sparring is where you have a free choice of attacking moves, but you are not attempting to score against your opponent. You take turns throughout the session attacking and defending. This gentle practice allows both partners to utilize attacking and defending moves in equal measures.

FULL-CONTACT SPARRING

In full-contact sparring, students will often wear full-body padding to protect their ribs from taking too many punishing blows.

Finally, there is free sparring, which is like a contest. This is the opportunity to put into practice all the skills you have developed throughout the rest of your training. You will usually spar with people of your own grade, but do not be afraid to take on someone of a higher grade—or even someone better than you. This is when you will improve the most: by forcing yourself to raise your skill level. By the same token, when sparring with lower grades, do not take the opportunity to thrash your partner. Use these practices to work on some of the weaker parts of your taekwondo skills or to develop new skills.

CONDITIONING YOUR ATTACK WEAPONS

Having toughened up your body for sparring, you will also need to toughen up your striking weapons for breaking. It will hurt a little the first time you attempt to break boards with your feet, but that is nothing compared to the pain experienced the first time you try to break boards with your hands or knuckles.

Toughening up your knuckles is easy. For this, you can do push-ups on them, either with the backs of your hands facing forwards or with them facing to the side. Make sure you put your weight on the first two knuckles, as these are the ones you strike with. This exercise will be uncomfortable and difficult at first, but remember, perseverance is one of the five tenets of taekwondo.

The ridges of your hands and feet and the balls of your feet will toughen up gradually over time, with lots of breaking practice, but not before you suffer a few blisters. Sore feet and hands will also become a feature of your life for a little while, but that is what you must put up with if you want to be able to take part in those amazing breaking feats seen at demonstrations. Traditionally, the Koreans have some fairly harsh methods of conditioning their hands and feet, using hot rocks and sacks of rice or bamboo shoots tied together. This tends to result in the disfiguration of the hands and feet, however, and so you should not try an exercise like this without first discussing it with your instructor.

HAVING FUN

The most important thing in taekwondo training, or indeed any martial arts training, is to have fun and enjoy yourself. Some people derive great enjoyment from pushing themselves to their limit, whereas others just enjoy progressing or the fitness and social aspects of being part of a club. People often attach a certain aura or mystique to martial arts and wrongly believe them to be inaccessible.

This is not the case—martial arts are for everyone. And taekwondo is no different from any other art in that respect. On a personal level, I have practiced and trained with some people who are among the most

PRESS-UPS

Taekwondo students are often encouraged to do press-ups on their knuckles to help toughen them up for destruction purposes. By hardening the skin around the knuckles, a student will feel less pain when punching hard boards or bricks.

TIGER TWINS

Taekwondo has featured heavily in the martial arts scenes on both the big screen and television. Two of the leading figures in this taekwondo revolution are the Tiger Twins—Master James Kim and Master Simon Kim. The twin brothers have appeared alongside some of the great names of martial arts movies, such as Jean-Claude Van Damme and Steven Seagal. They have also appeared with Tia Carrera in *Relic Hunter* and Chuck Norris in *Walker, Texas Ranger*. It is exposure such as this that has helped to elevate taekwondo to a position as one of the most popular martial arts practiced in America and across the world.

uncoordinated, unathletic, and naturally ungifted in sport I have ever come across. But they found fulfilment and enjoyment in taekwondo by progressing at their own levels.

Progress is not defined by stature or standing within a club or organization; it is defined by relative development according to your own abilities and potential. And where taekwondo stands out as an art for everyone is in its concentration on patterns. For this area of the art focuses on application and the desire to attain self-actualization and self-fulfilment. The pursuit of the coveted black belt is a journey, not a destination—a means, not an end.

Whatever your reasons for taking up taekwondo, you should do it because it gives you something extra in your life. Whether that is enjoyment, confidence, self-assurance, or friendship, you should practice taekwondo because it improves your life and improves you as a person. It does not matter what level you get to. Find a level that you are comfortable with, and then just take part in what is a highly rewarding martial art.

BREAKING

The main method of conditioning your hands and feet for destruction is to practice it. At first, it will hurt, but after a while, the hands and feet get used to it.

Glossary

Aikido   "Way of spirit or harmony"; Japanese martial art on which hapkido is largely based

Anaerobic   Relating to an activity in which the body requires more oxygen

Annex   To incorporate a country or other territory within the domain of a state

Bout   An athletic match

Cireum   A traditional Korean form of wrestling that has roots in Mongolian wrestling

Dan   The denomination of black-belt grades

Dobok   Taekwondo uniform

Dojang   Practice hall

Hapkido   "The way of harmony"; a Korean martial art encompassing throwing, joint locks, and weaponry, as well as taekwondo techniques

Hwarang   "The flowering manhood"; a group of martial artists trained in subak, taekyon, and cireum who were charged with protecting the kingdom of Silla from its enemies

Jirugi   Punching techniques

Kup   The denomination of taekwondo grades, from beginner to black belt

Makgi   Block

Pilsung   Modern patterns; also known as sabang hyung

Propriety   Correctness of behavior or morals

Sabang hyung	Modern patterns; also known as pilsung
Sogi	Stances
Spar	To practice fighting; this term is usually used with boxing
Subak	Ancient Korean martial art that inspired the founding of taekwondo
Taekyon	Foot fighting; an ancient forerunner of taekwondo
Taerigi	Striking techniques

Clothing and Equipment

CLOTHING

Gi: The gi is the most typical martial arts "uniform." Usually in white, but also available in other colors, it consists of a cotton thigh-length jacket and calf-length trousers. Gis come in three weights: light, medium, and heavy. Lightweight gis are cooler than heavyweight gis, but not as strong. The jacket is usually bound at the waist with a belt.

Belt: Belts are used in the martial arts to denote the rank and experience of the wearer. They are made from strong linen or cotton and wrap several times around the body before tying. Beginners usually wear a white belt, and the final belt is almost always black.

Hakama: A long folded skirt with five pleats at the front and one at the back. It is a traditional form of clothing in kendo, iaido, and jujutsu.

Zori: A simple pair of slip-on sandals worn in the dojo when not training to keep the floor clean.

WEAPONS

Bokken: A bokken is a long wooden sword made from Japanese oak. Bokken are roughly the same size and shape as a traditional Japanese sword (katana).

Jo: The jo is a simple wooden staff about 4–5 ft (1.3–1.6 m) long and is a traditional weapon of karate and aikido.

Kamma: Two short-handled sickles used as a fighting tool in some types of karate and jujutsu.

Tanto: A wooden knife used for training purposes.

Hojo jutsu: A long rope with a noose on one end used in jujutsu to restrain attackers.

Sai: Long, thin, and sharp spikes, held like knives and featuring wide, spiked handguards just above the handles.

Tonfa: Short poles featuring side handles, like modern-day police batons.

Katana: A traditional Japanese sword with a slightly curved blade and a single, razor-sharp cutting edge.

Butterfly knives: A pair of knives, each one with a wide blade. They are used mainly in kung fu.

Nunchaku: A flail-like weapon consisting of three short sections of staff connected by chains.

Shinai: A bamboo training sword used in the martial art of kendo.

Iaito: A stainless-steel training sword with a blunt blade used in the sword-based martial art of iaido.

TRAINING AIDS

Mook yan jong: A wooden dummy against which the martial artist practices his blocks and punches and conditions his limbs for combat.

Makiwara: A plank of wood set in the ground used for punching and kicking practice.

Focus pads: Circular pads worn on the hands by one person, while his or her partner uses the pads for training accurate punching.

PROTECTIVE EQUIPMENT

Headguard: A padded, protective helmet that protects the wearer from blows to the face and head.

Joint supports: Tight foam or bandage sleeves that go around elbow, knee, or ankle joints and protect the muscles and joints against damage during training.

Groin protector: A well-padded undergarment for men that protects the testicles and the abdomen from kicks and low punches.

Practice mitts: Lightweight boxing gloves that protect the wearer's hands from damage in sparring, and reduce the risk of cuts being inflicted on the opponent.

Chest protector: A sturdy shield worn by women over the chest to protect the breasts during sparring.

Further Reading

Corcoran, John and Emil Farkas. *Martial Arts: Traditions, History, People.* New York: Gallery Books, 1983.

Corder, Jason. *Taekwon-do: From White Belt to Yellow Belt.* London: Carlton Books, 2001.

Crompton, Paul. *The Complete Martial Arts.* London: Transworld Publishers, 1989.

Lewis, Peter. *Martial Arts.* London: Apple Press Ltd, 1988.

Mitchell, David. *The Complete Book of Martial Arts.* New York: Gallery Books, 1993.

Stepan, Charles A. *Taekwondo: The Essential Guide to Mastering the Art.* London: New Holland Publishers, UK Ltd., 2002.

Useful Web Sites

World Taekwondo Federation
http://www.wtf.org

International Taekwondo Federation
http://www.itf-taekwondo.com

Korean Taekwondo Association
http://www.koreataekwondo.org

European Taekwondo Union
http://www.etutaekwondo.org

United States Taekwondo Union
http://www.ustu.org

ITF Canada
http://www.ctfi.org

British Union of Taekwondo Federations
http://www.butf.com

ITF Australia
http://itfaustralia.com

ITF New Zealand
http://itfnz.org.nz

About the Author

Barnaby Chesterman is a 1st-dan black belt and has studied judo for more than 20 years. He is the official journalist for the International Judo Federation and has travelled all over the world to cover judo tournaments, including the Olympic Games in Sydney. As a journalist, Barnaby has worked for Reuters and several national broadsheet newspapers in the U.K. He has also participated in taekwondo and Thai boxing, and is a qualified judo coach.

Index

References in italics refer to illustration captions